The Right Madness on Skye

The Right Madness on Skye

Poems

Richard Hugo

W. W. NORTON & COMPANY
NEW YORK · LONDON

Some of these poems appeared in the following publications:

American Poetry Review, Field, Mississippi Review, The New Republic, The Seattle Review
"Druid Stones at Kensaleyre" and "Graves in Uig" originally appeared in *Antaeus*.

"The Right Madness on Skye" and "Villager" originally appeared in *The Atlantic Monthly*. Copyright © 1979, by The Atlantic Monthly Company, Boston, Mass. Reprinted with permission.

"The Clouds of Uig" and "Duntulm Castle" originally appeared in *The Hudson Review*.

"Ness" and "The Standing Stones of Callanish" originally appeared in *The Nation*.

"Clachard," "Piping to You on Skye from Lewis," and "Uig Registrar" originally appeared in *New England Review*. Reprinted by permission from *New England Review*, Vol. I, No. 4 (Summer, 1979). Copyright © 1979 by Richard Hugo.

"Greystone Cottage" and "St. Clement's: Harris" originally appeared under the title, "St. Clement's Church: Harris, Outer Hebrides" in *The New Yorker*, copyright 1978, 1979, respectively, The New Yorker Magazine, Inc.

"Ferniehirst Castle" and "Mill at Romesdal" originally appeared in *Poetry*.

Library of Congress Cataloging in Publication Data

Hugo, Richard F
   The right madness on Skye.

   1. Skye—Poetry.   I. Title.
PS3515.U3R5   811'.54   79-28051
ISBN 0-393-01353-7
ISBN 0-393-00982-3 pbk.

            1 2 3 4 5 6 7 8 9 0

Contents

Much thanks to the Guggenheim Foundation
for the chance to live on Skye and work
on these poems

The Semi-Lunatics of Kilmuir

And so they cheated and wandered and were loved
throughout this island. If that's too mythical a tone
consider those who conform and know something's wrong
and need a zany few who won't obey.
Granted, without obedience most of us would die,
and it was worse then, year eighteen whatever,
the crofts in feudal domain. Think of losing your home
on a Duke's whim and look at the home you lost.
Imagine this lovely island warped ugly by tears.

Yesterday in Glasgow some magistrate ruled
feudal rights prevail. Crofter reform turns out
a cruel joke. You pay and pay and own nothing.
Wouldn't we welcome them back this minute,
those clowning con men from Kilmuir?
They were crazy like dolphins. When Gilleasbuig Aotram,
most dolphin of all, met a real crazy
raving in chains, headed for the asylum, he said:
"Had you the right madness bread would be secure."
Have the right madness. This land has always passed on
and, like you, is still here.

*The Right Madness
on Skye*

A Snapshot of Uig in Montana

Children take longer to die
where sea hooks blue behind the headland
and the hooked dock longs for the next boat.
We will live there soon. The headless specter
moans the music all moan dispossessed.
Montana wants to be warmer and forget
how many farmed too hard and failed.
Most of all, here we want the self discarded
left unresurrected and wind resolved to move on.

There, we'll welcome both wind and dead air.
Look how hayricks though erect in rows
can't be soldiers and sky fights to stay blue.
To be old and charming as those fields
we must survive sad moments, must go on ploughing
after the invaders sail, all we love left broken
or dead: lamb, hut and barbarians' wake.
No sense waiting on the shore, fresh bread,
fresh tears. They're not coming back.

April and our snow hangs on. Whatever's
delaying spring rides high in arctic currents
and can't be controlled or explained.
In this shot of Uig, we can see all cause is local,
all effect. When we ask the way to Loch Sianta,
even if we've stopped the water horse
returned to terrorize the village, when he sees
we're foreign he'll put on his crofter's face
and where he points that will really be the trail.

A Map of Skye

We'll be confined and free. Roads end fast
and water leads slow ways to open water.
The harsh names on this map are Nordic,
the soft words Gaelic. We can love there well
grateful what is cruel ran out.
Even ruins will be civil, moss on ruins,
anger drained from ghost.
The only irritants, a soft longing for mist to clear
and a nagging feeling more should happen.

It's happened already. That will be the charm.
Not one isolated Indian war, relatively recent
and forgotten, but Celtic memory way back,
primal things to hate kept smouldering. . . .
England, Viking, the ninth century storm
that leveled farm and tower, and the tower down
the day of the invasion. It is all here
in the names, the sound of broken bone and blood.

We need that land of slow recovery, the grief passed
wife to daughter, some continuum of song
and we need bays that contain,
that promise a wider world beyond
the final promontory, as if travel
still involves the unknown. Read the roads.
A lot of switchbacks and a lot of time to find Portree.
And read the water, how salmon glow like swords
and checkpoints never run out.

Clachard

Maybe they believed anything that solid
and big must have eyes and would warn them
when Vikings sailed into view. We know
nothing about it, this stone stood on end.
Why on this spot? That much weight
took many men to erect we are certain.
In hard wind we imagine men crushed
under the stone and the trying again.
In soft light we see horses and rope.
When modern and think we think ancient,
we say phallic symbol or breast.
Tired we say God and tower guard.
Let them know we are strong. After we love
we say it's a signal to birds: come home.
It occurs to the poor, this is a sign
of surrender. To any invader, it said:
sail in and take me. And says it today.
After awhile you'll forget why you came.
In time you won't know what I say.

Greystone Cottage

Some days the tick of two protestant clocks
in the cottage, related in some nebulous no less
real way to one long ago, put me again
at the kitchen window waiting for rain.
Open bright sky, and I look across Uig bay
and *ru Chorachan* to the river cascading
nine miles away down the Waternish cliff
into Loch Snizort. At one time, Iain,
our neighbor, our friend, tells me, salmon
clustered under that steady pelt of fresh water
on salt year long for the illegal taking.
I dream myself poacher. I dream myself
benevolent wealthy invader, nothing on board
but my need to be welcome ashore.
I bring you songs from a glamorous planet.

The rooms are small and built so that sound
cannot carry one to another. Alone in a room
as I am now in the kitchen, the house seems empty
and I hear only one clock. Anger cannot carry
nor laughter. How I feel is locked in with me.
I could be dying and no one would hear my cry:
'Call Doctor MacRae.' I could spot a ship of threat
sailing in, ancient Viking, modern American oil.
No one would hear my warning throughout the house,
throughout the island. Like salmon
we wait to be taken. Nothing will save this peace,
this near sacred space between people and homes.

This is the season hayricks dot crofts
and hotels shut down and the English tourist
goes back to London. We're staying on, snug
in our cottage, snug alone in each room.
The clock in the kitchen reminds me of a time
few people dropped by and all mattered.
Rain on the window reminds me when
a vagabond in rags came looking for odd jobs.
He sang to himself and I still remember the tune.

The Clouds of Uig

Over the years these clouds have colored much
cloud white and blue: horse, house and fence,
the recent tower already in ruin.
They change the green of Skye apple to Kelly
and back a hundred times a day.
They never stop changing the distance to the pier
from your front door.

They have no form. No one would mistake
the shade of one on water for a boat.
They never slow down and they never run out.
When one sky leaves, taking with it the rain
that couldn't make anyone wet or leave grass
dry very long, another sky follows close behind,
the loud blue interval between. . . .
recess in a crowded school.

They move on like your students, sixty years
of them and still they come
like surly children, like amorphous rules of light
we can't quite understand and have to obey.
A new set of rules this minute, faintly the same.
We can live under them.
They move certain as blood. Under their shade
the bay locks complete and, deep in that cloudy water,
many lives go on.

for Johan Ross

16

Graves in Uig

The dead are hidden from the sea. The sea
can't find them on this high moor over
on the inland slope where stones aren't kept up
and grass goes uncut and sheep wander where they please
among the stones dropping their olive pit black turds.
Sixty-eight stones in all counting blank markers
and no more than nine names, most of them
starting with M. Some stones count for more than one
and one spans decades between
the first name on it dead and the last.

I have a theory. It's not good but hear me.
East and north are the cold winds. Right?
And the west wind brings rain and holds
temperature in check. I say they put the dead
here where north and east gales can find them,
knowing in death we are tough, and leave the living
on the west side protected from cold.

I admit one fenced off large stone is obscured
by brush and the iron grillwork around it
has rusted, one section already down. That
makes you think, doesn't it, someone lost interest
over the years, or the dead left a last request
to leave them alone? One other theory I have
involves women never heard of on this island
and has nothing to do with the dead.

We walked here, my wife and I, this day
vivacious in sunlight. Last night
we heard about the death of Robert Lowell.
You pass through two gates to get here.
Both are very much in working order.

Hawk in Uig

Every good wind he hangs over the field
in front of our cottage. Head on he looks like a bat.
Bela Lugosi's returned, I say. My wife
doesn't laugh, nor my daughter. Twelve minutes
almost to the second he hangs
then veers off
back into his life of circle and search.

The wind up, if he's not here by ten
I know something's wrong with the current,
water or air. When he dives he seems to have
no mackerel in mind.
I suspect he's always at play, like a swallow
no reason for his movements other than fun
despite his stern face and his eye full of hot hunger.

I knew a family back home so ugly
I still think of them. I was young and cruel
and made fun of the daughter's bad looks
and her three dumb looking brothers, mouths open
in effort to understand the nothing
and bad something that were both bound to happen.
I don't remember their name. I remember
it sounded shabby and poor like them.

The hawk hasn't shown today. The wind
doesn't seem weak and the sea bangs the cliff
as it always does when he comes. Past two now
and no sign. Rain hits the window
with an empty sound and runs down

obscuring the view. Clearing now
and still no hawk. I'm weak waiting.
I promise the sky tomorrow if he comes
I'll call him something better than Bela
and I'll offer him meat.

Uig Registrar

No in-between. The news is good or bad
and hard to write in a neutral hand—
died of exposure, 4 A.M., 40 yards from home—
body not recovered—cause not ascertained—
wed, church of Scotland—19 and 22.
Cold in words. Flat in lasting ink.
Some come elated, the sad long history
of Scotland shed for the moment. Some
come heavy with recent loss and with
that dignity they took from Celtic stone.
You write it down. Below, the Rha
and Conon enter the bay. You try
to catch the hum of their steady entry
beyond the choked phrase, the bridal smile.
You write it down, the way it has to be
for the record, the way it has to be.

for Chatta MacLean

Piping to You on Skye from Lewis

Pipe the Gaelic back for one last dance.
One long war over, you took a private vow:
say goodbye to islands only once.

Honor them daily with music, those dead attendants
of the fate of living Gaels: to lose.
Pipe the dead Gaels back for one more dance.

In war you might die English, might get buried in Provence.
Best concentrate on what the Skye dead did and do—
say goodbye to islands only once.

Goodbye home you said to Bragar, there's a bony chance
bones stay whole in cairns. From Stornoway, your radio
pipes the dead Gaels back for one more dance

and you bend close to the static, convinced
you'll find in bagpipe overtones the drumming reason to
say goodbye to islands only once.

War's tough on personal reconnaissance.
Spy from this green distance on your life and pray you
say goodbye to islands only once.
Gaels who die at home show up for every dance.

for Iain MacLean

21

The Clearances

Lord, it took no more than the wave of a glove,
a nod of the head over tea. People were torn from their crofts
and herded aboard, their land turned over to sheep.
They sailed. They wept.
The sea said nothing and said I'll get even.
Their last look at Skye lasted one hour. Then fog.
Think of their fear. When you can't read, not even a map,
where does home end and Tasmania start?
Think of loss that goes stormy knots beyond bitter
and think of some absentee landlord home in his tower
signing the order and waving off a third ale.

Want an equation? O.K. The lovelier the land
the worse the dispossession. I know that's not right.
Blacks weep when put out of a shack,
Puerto Ricans to see the slum torn down.
We've all lost something or we're too young to lie,
to say we hear crofters sobbing
every high tide, every ferry that sails
Uig for Lewis, that vague shape out there in haze.
We don't hear them sob. We don't know that they did.
And that form in the haze might be nothing,
not a destination, no real promise of home.

Some afternoons when pressure builds in the bay
and I think the sea will explode one more
mile per hour of gale, I wave my hand
and have the ship abort. I bring them back
and say it was a mistake. The landlord was drunk.
He's happy you're here. Don't worry. I'll find room

for the sheep. They laugh loud as money
and sing back to their crofts. When water relaxes
into a lazy roll home, Lewis stark in clear air,
I know they'd come ashore the way they left,
numbed by hard labor and grim
and I'd be no friend in their flat eyes.

Glen Uig

Believe in this couple this day who come
to picnic in the Faery Glen. They pay rain
no matter, or wind. They spread their picnic
under a gale-stunted rowan. Believe they grew tired
of giants and heroes and know they believe
in wise tiny creatures who live under the rocks.

Believe these odd mounds, the geologic joke
played by those wise tiny creatures far from
the world's pitiful demands: make money, stay sane.
Believe the couple, by now soaked to the skin,
sing their day as if dry, as if sheltered inside
Castle Ewen. Be glad Castle Ewen's only a rock
that looks like a castle. Be glad for no real king.

These wise tiny creatures, you'd better believe,
have lived through it all: the Viking occupation,
clan torturing clan, the Clearances, the World War
II bomber gone down, a fiery boom
on Beinn Edra. They saw it from here. They heard
the sobs of last century's crofters trail off below
where every day the Conon sets out determined for Uig.
They remember the Viking who wandered off course,
under the hazelnut tree hating aloud all he'd done.

Some days dance in the bracken. Some days go out
wide and warm on bad roads to collect the dispossessed
and offer them homes. Some days celebrate addicts
sweet in their dreams and hope to share with them
a personal spectrum. The loch here's only a pond,
the monster in it small as a wren.

Believe the couple who have finished their picnic
and make wet love in the grass, the wise tiny creatures
cheering them on. Believe in milestones, the day
you left home forever and the cold open way
a world wouldn't let you come in. Believe you
and I are that couple. Believe you and I sing tiny
and wise and could if we had to eat stone and go on.

Sneosdal

What a walk. First mile uphill. The road
went rock to peat to mud. The final
five hundred yards we floundered through lumpy swamp.
Whatever we've read in old novels, it's no fun
to walk in heather, and we'd have to cut this wind
in half to enjoy a kiss on the moor.
We believe him worth it, the legend
of this loch: *Each uisge*, water-horse.
Hasn't he kept us in terror all our lives?
This is where he lives, in this eerie black water
tucked in behind the crag
that rises like a bad past between our faces
and all of the afternoon sun. We know his disguises:
gentleman of the evening, sheep dog, normal horse.
And we know he comes to our village for no reason
other than to frighten what we used to call maidens
or to kill the mayor
we've never been organized enough to elect.
He's not drunk with power. He comes
just now and then when least expected, when
we enjoy an innocent picnic
or go to the store. Sometimes
we think we see him and don't. A dog looks wrong
in certain light or one horse won't run with the others
exhilarated by gales. When we see a man,
white tie and tails, given our lives we know
that much charm is suspect. We lock our doors
when a lone hawk seems to enjoy the storm.
He hasn't come for so long, today we've tracked him

to his home. We had a hard time finding you.
We are wet and cold. The blackface sheep resent us.
The shepherd won't return our wave. With the world
on its way to certain disaster, can't you reappear,
rise slimy and majestic out of the loch and snort
at least one minor threat to keep us in line?
Or are we out of monsters? Are we now reduced
to sensible conclusion like empty water,
with no one more interesting than ourselves to fear?
We take the long walk back, mud to peat
to rock, the last mile easy downhill.
Our car has never waited for us this long before.
We are embarrassed by what we hold in,
the hopeful and hopeless child that wants to cry—
We saw him. We saw him. He is really there.

Kilmuir Cemetery: The Knight in Blue-Green Relief

The rotten thing is after you've been pushed around
so often over the years, moved near the gate
for visitor convenience, moved near Flora MacDonald
in effort to have all brave ones united,
not scattered here and there like in life,
and the current whether or not to keep you safe
in a museum, I can't be sure you mark the spot
the one you represent is buried: Angus of the Storms.
It shouldn't matter, but he was a knight in life
as you are in stone and we've run out of knights.

Is this where you belong? And were you really
that brave? Didn't you come home nervous
from war and have bad dreams loaded
with sobbing children and dead innocent sheep?
Didn't the tinkle of a far off cow bell though faint
explode you out of sleep?
Or were you always this resolute, the way you look now
on this slab flat in the grass, and were you always this
noble and aloof, paying no attention
to rain that pools in your eyes?

I knew a man so brave he flew extra missions
because he believed in the war. We called him
Screwy Jew, and his odds stretched thin until
one day he exploded into fine sand and fell
five miles in a trillion leisurely trails
no one cared to trace. Do you know him now?

Is he one of you? I imagine you asking for trouble
wherever you rode and cowardly peasants like me
moving out of your way. And I imagine you dead
on a beach and gulls collected to shade
your blood from drying too fast in the sun.
That was a great moment. We went on ploughing.

You here smug in blue green stone relief
may represent no one. If you were really that small
and took off your mail, put down your sword
and shield, I'd break your goddamn puny arms, I'd
knee you in the balls, I'd kick your ass north
all the way to the pole. They wouldn't carve me in stone,
nor call me Dick of the Storms. Something right goes wrong
with brutality when it loses history and style.
These days, however many dragons we kill
we are sand falling home
leaving no trail.

Kilmuir Cemetery: Stone with Two Skulls and No Name

Probably two thieves, but why a stone this big,
this thick horizontal slab? The time it must have taken
to carve those skulls. Who paid for that? Surely
it was not an elaborate lesson to others: don't steal.
And what could anyone steal that others would honor him
this much after he's hung? Doesn't work out at all.

Maybe one killer. The second skull his victim. There.
Remember the victim twice, once in his grave
and once here, and the murderer a brief once under this slab
heavy enough to hold him down forever. The problem remains.
Who paid for all this? Why not put
the killer's corpse on the beach and tell the sea-birds,
"Start picking." In this fresh air he couldn't reek long and in no time
his bones would be clean.

"And these two never touch in the air so full of summer"
a poet once said of two stones. One marked a woman.
The other a man. What if two lovers left a stipulation
in their will: they refused to die unless buried together.
And the state, not bright in those days either, agreed.
This is a northern island. There's no air here
so filled with summer we're better off in death alone.
The moon is never not always sometimes in Scandinavia
no matter how simple it sounds.
When you're a skeleton, it's hard to find a lover.
Take it with you, brother, sister. You'll find days
any old bony kiss will do.

Duntulm Castle

Those knights had an eye for strategic location.
One look at the sea and they knew the way danger
would come. What better than this, the ocean open
all the way to the sky. Only one island nearby
Tulm, and that with no cover. In this harmless
dramatic weather, what better place to wonder
what I would have been, cook or castle clown
or knave who stole out of need, a captive in the dungeon
scratching on stone one more year of the hundreds
I lost dying of slow darkness.

If you hear anything bad about me, believe it.
Given a choice, I'd be crofter, friend to anyone.
To the army that went out and the other army
that came back I'd wave the same good luck
and go on turning the dirt and planting. Time
for conscription, I'd say: look, without me, no food.
I'd manage to always stay here, my world cut short
by the stone fence I must not plant beyond.
Think anything you want in your castle
perfecting good manners. Old as I am, something
happens inside when gannets collapse their wings
and free fall into the waves like dead stars.
I excuse myself from wars.
You stand before me ferocious in armour and mail

and ridicule when I tell you the raven comes here
because damn it all he's a raven and this
is a castle in ruin. Sure, I'm afraid of your sword,
your unforgiving eyes. Haven't I begged
and begged at your gate for scraps in bad winters?

                              3

The same two herons flew the same formation then.
To me, that's fun. To knghts it meant spies
and a means of attack they'd not counted on.
Did I tell you I've flown and dropped bombs?
Buildings looked like you do now then.
I was handsome in my uniform.
That's about the time you gave the traitor
salted beef and salt water and laughed him dead of thirst.
I wish I was poet enough to hear his final gasp
from the dungeon, and man enough to admit it's just me.

                              4

Hard wind hates imagination. I come from a land
where without half trying we create
a thousand reasons to say goodbye. In this wind
I'm afraid to lean over the rim and watch the babe
fall inadvertently bye bye into the sea,
the nurse beside me begging "Don't tell them"
and the same nurse below tied to the prow
by her hair and tide coming in for an all time high.
Don't tell them over tea at the Duntulm Hotel.
I'm the one who told.

Once a year a poet came
on foot over the moor.
He read and they listened hard.
Year after year he came,
every time a little more welcome,
a little more polished.
In time he ate with the knights
and had his choice of the women.
Gradually, he relaxed.
One day he read a poem
that sang a way to get here
no knight had considered.
They banished him to Tulm.
Gulls took his bones
and one by one
dropped them into the sea.
So help me.

Mill at Romesdal

One look at this mill and the adjacent croft,
the local intimate way grass slants to the mill,
the sea beyond the broken water wheel, and we know
here we could keep some private promise to improve.
We could reinforce the floor
where grain was milled, repair the tracks
for the grain cart, redivert the small stream
back into the flume and start the mill again.
Send the word out now: your miller
is open to all who bring raw grain.

If we could turn our lives that way, the way
the mill stones turned, slow and even,
the milled grain falling dreamy all day
every day but Sunday into carts, we'd find
some recent peace, a composure we never quite trust
in family portraits. We'd be wise to allow
for the loch that hammers inside
and that man not on record who broke one day
in the byre and demanded the cattle say thanks.
With this loch pale in our faces and money
collected last year for milling turning
to dust at the touch, we really are happy, are happy—
our voices run down late summer,
the stream without pressure and the water wheel limp.

If we count bones found on Skye, we get
Celtic, a lot, Viking, very few, despite
three centuries of occupation and Nordic names
that hang on: Hinnisdal, Monkstadt, Eyre.

The Viking bones found here
don't care what we or the man they belonged to did.
They don't blush for their part in oppression,
innocent women in shock.
There's a way of saying, "Yes! We were rotten, so what?"
Of saying it any time we want to the sea
that answers softly in Gaelic and doesn't indict.

We won't restore the mill. The water wheel's
broken beyond repair and, if we got the two stones
back in gear and grinding, no one raises grain
today on this island. The modern Norwegian ship
needs papers to sail these waters. The Viking bones
are in Glasgow for date and classification.
We own the mill in the warmest sense of own.
Let's keep it run down. Let's keep the crofter's cottage
empty and cold. If anyone asks for a miller
we'll say, that's what we were once, and worse.
This is what we are now.

for Dr. Calum MacRae

Druid Stones at Kensaleyre

I imagine Druids timeless, so lacking
a sense of time that, like animals, they found
every moment loaded with now, and no future,
no, or too much, awareness of death. These two stones,
woman and man I'd guess, will age no faster
than the bay they overlook. Like all stone
they will stay young and know nothing.

Driving north from Portree, from a certain point
on the road the church at Kensaleyre
looks higher than the stones I say
are woman and man, and that seems wrong.
Sundays, a cleric lays on stone ears
modern concepts of sin. Stone throats don't tighten.
The sea doesn't listen. I, who don't go to church,
live alone with what I've done.

Some day I'll bypass the church and keep going
across the brief moor to where they stand,
that young couple, beautiful, poised.
I'll put out my hand and say my name.
They'll say "Welcome" in stone. If you pass
in your car and see three of us solid
forever above and one with the sea, despite the wear
of weather and the way indifferent traffic
hurts even the stoniest heart, know one
came late, is happy and won't be back.

The Braes

I would have taken this road on sight
not knowing who lived along it,
not knowing where, if anywhere, it goes.
I'd drive unaware Celt blood flows
even now in the grass, the result of violent gesture
against the injustice of seizure
by a callous feudal gentry,
imagining my entry
foreign, modern American, tame.
I'd drive this road for the same
old reason, to find a poem, drive
slowly by crofters who don't return the wave
of strangers, then use feeling alone
to follow some personal line
that won't do here where the first resistance
flared up and got the instant
result they fought for, the men and women.
They won and they won later in London.
Better I put a curse on Ballingall.
Roast, roast in the fires of hell.
Nothing here more than any place
else on this island says we faced
them here and bled. You have to know
this is where the poor woke up a nation.
Same time, back home, in sand, in snow
where nothing grows
we started Indian reservations.

for Sorley & Renee MacLean

St. John's Chapel

All debris ends here at the north end
of Loch Caroy where St. John's chapel
and a dozen graves sit below the road
unnoticed and summer traffic pours north
to Dunvegan, the clean castle there,
the informed guide. It must be wrong
to bury your dead where the sea forgets to be nice,
sits there sullen and every day deposits
one more afternoon of waste.

Wouldn't this try belief?
Could we fake faith when needing one word
of comfort we find the chapel locked forever,
our dead child's marker fallen over,
this sad beach littered with acres of trash?
And what good are flowers growing from graves
when we need to cry 'forget forget'
loud in this forgotten spot.

And we need to take note of the grillwork.
The iron fence that should surround the dead
broke apart like an afterthought.
Rats have their way at night.
Names on stone got lost in the gnaw and crawl
of moss. If we clawed a faded name
and sobbed 'is this, is this the one?'
it would come out flat.

We want severed connections.
We want the ocean trailing off out

of the void of lost promise and rage
into this bay and that, some lovely,
some, like this one, sick. With water, with number
of graves we feel the urge to be finite.

No telling why we stopped. Our dead
are buried continents away, in cemeteries
well kept up with money, stones relatively
recent, names in clean relief.
Maybe the stairs seduced us, the climb down
out of sight of cars that catch the sun
once and move on.

Trumpan

It just says 'church' on the map.
No mention of fire, the MacDonalds gloating downwind,
the MacLeods in mid-hymn burning.
Their screams ran away
to silence in the west roar of air.
This is that same loud air. This day,
despite the storm seems quiet, the view pastoral
even where land falls off
sudden as life and sea snarls below us like white hair.

The sky's a calendar shot: clouds
rationing light and light streaming down
one shaft to spotlight one green patch
of water in the dark forever. Sing
herring boats home, good wife.
Your voice, quiet as love, rides the right wind right
to where the radio waits for the forecast,
the rare true heading to port.

With no towns, with villages so thin
vacant lots outnumber homes fifty or more
to one, and fences try to convince the deafening storm
they know the property line, all we brought,
food, wine and attitude, must be consumed
in a quick chaotic picnic. We can't talk
until we're in the car and in the car we don't.

Home in Uig, we count the boats. All here.
All men accounted for. In the whole of Skye
no one died today. Make room in dreams
for Trumpan. Remember a road that goes to murder
and comes back friend.

Langaig

We are what we hear. A well known singer died
yesterday in Spain. Thirty-five years ago
I got fired for sneaking off to hear him. I sobbed
"sorry" at the foreman, fired days later himself.
I cast blue nylon high over water turned black
by peat and light diminished by heavy Highland low sky.
I heard music and lost my job. I've not worked hard since
on anything but words, though I fish all waters
devoted and hum old songs when I fish alone.

I hum "My Heart is Taking Lessons," a song
the dead singer sang. I hum "I Had the Words and You
in My Heart." I remember him singing that.
I hum flat and off key, but that's hardly my fault,
the lack of gift, of training. In this lake (read 'loch'
to be local) trout run black as the water though Scots
like us call them 'browns,' the old Scots, 'Loch Leven!'
I hum "Makes No Difference Now," the best recording
the dead singer made and he left lots of good records.

To relax, to slide with, ride the forces of whatever
sweeps us along, jokes well timed, phrasing under control—
that was my ideal. I didn't come close in real life.
A soft impulse was proof I was weak. I laughed
at any weak joke, still do, and believed our purpose
to lighten the day, to be tougher than fate.
In reaction to that, I believed we should give in to pathos.
Today I believe: fish hard and hum every tune
I remember hearing the dead singer sing

and leave believing in being like him to others.
Does that make us brothers? Let's be. My bobber
jitters and I know it isn't just wind. I set my line
too soon and lose the black brown. The eagle yells
from the Quirang, "Go easy. Give him time to take it."
I hum "White Christmas," though I never liked it.
Snow on mainland mountains across the minch (if you're
American read 'strait') reminds me I'm fishing
late in the season. I may be breaking Scot law.

Christ, what rain and no real Jesus in it.
No real king. No friend. What lover first inserted a tongue
in a lover's ear? And where? It must have been pre-
Peloponesian war. It must have been pre-all
language and hunger, and located song prior to lyrics.
Fishing preceded song. We know that from instinct,
not records. I've fished this loch often before
and alone with my ghosts felt free to sing.
I've got a brown on. My line is writing a song.

I'm fishing. I'm singing. My heart is not exactly
giving lessons though I've been lucky enough in rare
moments to take heart in some words, and to have
a job teaching others to sing, to locate by game
some word like 'brown' in black water, to cast
hard for that word, then wait a long time to set.
Now the reeling in, the fight, the black trout lovely
on heather, the dead singer in songs
we recover, and hum when alone, and hum wrong.

Ayr

You might die anywhere. You will die in Ayr
north of the river, in the Newton Cafe.
You'll die to no notice in the Orient Cinema
in the balcony.

When you die in Ayr, if you die
in the Newton Cafe, jars of good cheap candy
on shelves back of the counter
will remind the investigating officer of home.

If you die in the Orient Cinema
George C. Scott will not be on the screen,
not at your final moment.
The janitor will find you. No reaction.

South of the river the town of Ayr's alive.
New shops. New shopping center. The tongue
will be braid at the inquest.
You won't understand.

The next town north is Prestwick. Big international
airport. BOAC as usual, late.
Whoever was coming to visit will say
he's not here. Where is he?

You'll die in Ayr
where warehouses rent for next to nothing
and rats complain, no rats other than them.
The report will read: not from here.

The report will read: foreigner, deceased.
The investigating officer

will ask the girl back of the counter at the Newton Cafe
to a movie.

Visitors will make their way to Glasgow.
Scotland is not bewildering.
People are helpful. The food is uninteresting.
Lots of castles in beautiful ruin.

Try Ayr in the off-season. Try
the Newton Cafe some early winter evening.
Scampi and chips. Try staring
out the window at some earlier street.

Don't try dying. I just said that to mention
Ayr. In the Orient a couple holds hands
and George C. Scott shows them how to act.
Try Ayr north of the river. Try some earlier home.

Ferniehirst Castle

This was our first line of defense. It held
about five minutes. What could we throw at them?
A few chickens to trip over, a cow to block the road,
and one farmer who didn't want anyone hurt.
Sheep and maze remained neutral.
The priest who worked the chapel changed a few
key names in the sermon and went on.

Was there ever a better place to let the enemy through
and years later when he came back enroute home
to act as if nothing had changed?
Nothing has changed. Did you have trouble
fording the Jedwater river? Was there
a one eyed farmer, not quite right in the head?
He died. Come in and get warm.
Stay here until you are strong enough to go on.

Centuries have passed since then, all of them
just as bad. The sermon changed this way
and that and couldn't keep up with the times.
Despite architectural plans, rooks know
this castle will go to ruin. When they come for good
as they always do when they find broken stone,
they'll spend their lives on basics, searching for food
and flapping dark signals to the man taking notes.

We do best with short range plans,
so limited rooks take off bewildered.
In any century, to stay humane we lived
in one or another kind of isolation, far as we could

from highway and harm. Even then,
too much ocean too long or forest, our eyes
started to see things and our blood turned to rain.
This is very old mortar. If we do this and not that
to the floor and don't get too smart with the ceiling
all who return with very old hurt in their eyes
will know they are welcome.

for Chester Kerr

Culloden

Nothing seems right, not the monument too close
to the road nor the road that seems misplaced.
We'd have everyone fallen named, not one stone
per clan, hidden in fern or behind a cedar,
even the clan name faint, and trails that wander
the woods better for lovers than for tribute.
We can't imagine trumpets, the steel clash of men,
the bonnie prince riding away. If anything
we think of picnics, cold salmon and wine.

If a hill isn't rounded some filmatic way
could anyone bleed there, could a fifteen year
old boy cry 'Mother, I'm dying' then die?
We need wind to fight wars. No wind here.
The air's too dead for the dead. The trees too solemn
for contrast with a serious tear of defeat.

We have to trust books and the handed down
stories of loss. Otherwise, given this sun
breaking clean on the grass, museums meant
to commemorate mean nothing. We have to trust
the faces of Scots today, the pulse of blood
in those faces. And we have to trust the sad
memorial tone of anyone who volunteers
to guide us through this field not right for battle.
We say, yes, yes, we hear the pipes, the drums.
We see the charge. We hear the fatal screams.

We are simply being polite. No topography
lends itself easily to war. To animals maybe.
To birds. To clouds. A grave we hope to outlive.

The Standing Stones of Callanish

See them in snow under a full moon they told me.
The shadows will take you out of yourself to when
the Stones were erected, the time it took and the reason
we try to guess today. Some claim, a way to tell time.
Others say, religion. I guess pattern itself,
the delight of pattern and, if we ride birds,
center, circle and spoke looked down on lovely.
Contrast it with uncertain currents of sea,
gales that rip up what seemed
well rooted rock and send flying like suicidal stars.
These stones wear better than sky. See
the clouds in tatters and blue faded to weak cream
at noon with no explanation. Gales clear the grounds
of brochures torn in frustration at phrases—
'the dates are unknown'—'Herodotus states Abaris
told Ptolemy'—when? I try
to remember history and can't get past World War I.
I've walked around them twice, December in my bones,
knelt to get an angle on the two long rows
going north from the hub, one direction I've always believed.
And I've calculated the weight of the big one
and guessed the number of men it took and the work
to bring it from Wales where some say it's from,
a special barge that wobbled and rode high without cargo,
and that special day they put it in place and it settled
the way they'd hoped and it held. That was long before
people knew how to cheer, shake hands or offer a toast.

I imagine them resting a moment, then grim with resolve
starting down to the sea to get the next stone,
and one woman thought strange but obeyed,
urging them on and muttering hard at the sky
a word we've lost. It sounded like 'shape.' It meant 'world.'

Ness

This is where those who hate monuments
pay last disrespects to the world. They've wrecked art,
cities, the language passed woman to man and back.
They've destroyed personal records, birth, school, marriage
and divorce. With luck they'll board a final ship
that flies a flag no color on earth.
They'll bribe the captain to destroy the record of death.
For them the horizon is a pass.
Beyond it the glamour and thrill of ignorant waste.

And I'll be one of them, no shame. I'll tear every poem
and toss lines in tatters to that great God, wind.
I'll leave laughing. Everything ends here: life,
hope, civilization, love, loneliness and regret. The end
promised children. The world on medieval maps
that drops off blue for water into white for void.
I'll give up whatever's hard, saying the plural of ghost,
the singular of girls.
I'll shed my life and sail counter to breakers.

The ship will tire far out and lose stroke and start back
in the wash. On my way home I'll dream it again,
something like history even if wrong, starting with sun
and coming down the ages, unclassified tooth
to computer, star to diamond and back. If you find me
broken and babbling on rock, listen very hard.
The tongue may be dated. If you pick up a phrase
you can match it with words on that scrap of paper.
You found it in Wind. You don't worship wind any more.

Carloway Broch

Park. Let's walk the brief path back
1600 years across the field
to where we once lived. When we left we carefully
left no record. To reach old age, 25,
we built the doorway low and posted a guard,
rock in each hand, over the entrance
the enemy, whoever he was, would have to crawl.
If woman with child, you slept high
on the elevated tier of stone slabs we wedged
between the two walls. If man, on the ground
in case of attack. No attack came.
We grew up guessing which man was father.
That didn't matter as much as fire
or fish we took from the sea.

By 400 A.D., we'd gone. Most of us
dead and the few who remained called Celt.
We were innocent prey to concept:
God, family, cross. Within two centuries
we'd upped the ante to 30,
moved out of the broch and into stone huts.

Let me skip 14 centuries or so.
You can find those in books.

And you can see what happened to home, most
of the old stone gone, at least two thirds
of the double wall down and what remains,
some tribute to our skill, we call "ruin"
or "historic shrine." By now the fish
we called "food" swim named. Local animals seem

too small for those skins we slept on and this sky
full of rockets and space program debris
tightens the eye. After we lived here we lived
many places and lives—none of our doing really—
mostly result of war. This century alone one war
took 50 million. We could not believe it then—
that world with so few souls and we huddled here,
one community, 20, every hard gale.

Bastard, also a concept, is considered obscene.
Given my genes, my medical past and my recent
ability to control bad habits
I expect to reach 83. Wife, children, friend—
I want you along all the way. Let's walk
the stone hard trail ahead to where we are now,
beside the car looking back at what we were.
The broch towering over the farm
silhouettes itself against the ever climbing sea
and the ever diminishing sky.

We say "beautiful" and don't know why.

The Cairn in Loch An Duin

Is this all we will know of the dark,
bone dark under rock and just out
of dry reach? This black water lake
that supposes no trout, now and then catches
blue fire under a quick passing gap in the clouds.
It must have been planned, the cairn
set just beyond our wading range,
some message understood: leave us alone.
Leave them alone. Don't ask in Bragar
the date of the cairn.

We guess a spirit wants out from under
the rock. One aching jawbone cries to come ashore,
to climb the short hill to Bragar
and sit there with other old Celts and chat.
What would he tell us of time, of long days grinding
across the sky without us? Do some clouds repeat
like planets? Any improvements in food?
And we'd ask him one question that burns:
Dead, will we, without going mad
envy the town we see every day and can't enter?

Death may be weaker than sleep. We know flesh
rejoins water and dirt, and for centuries believed
the soul unites with the sky. The memory
would find some special other place, a gold cottage
that houses all we were, are and will be, high on a moor
over the open ocean, where wind slams home
and a child cries excited.
Can't we be more than just bone under this plain pile

of rock in a lake close to shore,
the living tauntingly near?

In Bragar a whale jaw forms an arch
and through it the living pass to market.
That giant bone reminds us more than the cairn
of what's left behind one darkening moment—
rain, music and tongue.
This is where sky bears down
year after year and light ranges dim
to dim blinding. We're left with whatever
we find inside to keep going.
Bones mix in the cairn.

The water flames blue and beyond the cairn
one ripple. We can bait a hook,
can cast and wait. This is no song of reprieve.
The small jaw stays locked in stone.
The whale jaw opens wider in the town.
The surface fills with ripple. We cry
"trout, trout, trout" to each other. Hard. Honor the trout
this season honor goes lonely as bones.
They play the surface like children,
what we have been.

St. Clement's: Harris

Lord, I'd rehearsed and rehearsed your loss.
You died and my rehearsed face, the words
I'd planned to say over your stone were ready.
I set my face. I said my words. The sea I worship
did nothing to relieve the grief in Rodel.
This day, December 28, 1977,
the church locked, I bang the door and no one comes.
Happy New Year, Lord. Almost that time.

We were something else that age of reptiles.
The triwinged dragonfly drove us to caves.
There we huddled and shook. Those days, all
huge creatures, dinosaur and those that end in –saurus,
no matter how imposing meant less than land.
For one example: white cliffs climbed
so straight they seemed geometry
and high high when we looked gave off
gratuitous white light that formed, fragmented,
floated and was cloud. I'm afraid
the introverted palm leaves even then
threatened to open and smile. The world would bloom
with or without us. Every dawn, the sky
turned pink like special places on girls.
No Lord then, we were something else. O.K.?

Three days and this year ends. Nothing's touched
after five hundred years. Brochures with photos
taken in some rare good weather
don't mention dead reptiles. Here it started
with man, woman and with what they believed

and couldn't understand. Christ came on so northern
he wore skins. Believe and fish will come.
If I was terminal and had six weeks and knew it
I'd fish every lake on Harris. That's a lot
of water. And I'd fake faith long enough
to leave room on my stone for favorable words.
I'd fish the ocean hard my last day on this page.

To get down to earth, if buried here
with faith—even in death we love beauty—
I'd be buried redeemed. Look,
the ocean below and forever, the wide void void
of eternity's nightmare, the lovely way
graves are spaced to leave room for grass.
The date of my death would endure
given good stone and some artisan's fine tools.
May he carve "decent" despite what came out at the inquest.
Please understand, that was just a bad time.
If I can't enter the church, at least
I can go on peeking. Inside, shadows
fall like jail from leaded windows wrong onto stone.

Lord, you're dead. Imagine five centuries gone
and me far as sky from ruin. Imagine
this locked church and my pounding, my hope
to study six hundred year old carvings inside.
Like anyone
I come from a monstrous age, white cliffs
climbing and climbing out of whatever painting
I saw once, climbing out of the frame
and somewhere above
issuing light that released became
some aimless immediate plural.

Letter to Garber from Skye

Dear Fred: I hope this finds you, Marge and children O.K.
We're living on Skye, in Uig, in a homey cottage
high over the bay. Below us, two rivers, the Conon
and Rha enter the sea. Both look trouty and aren't, a trick
peat plays staining the water dark brown and mysterious
where the rivers begin high on the moor. It's windy nearly
all the time, and when you look out the window you think
it's cold. You go out and it isn't. The people too are like that.
Warmer than you think on first sight, with no throw-away charm
like in cities. The sky, water, vegetation and wind are Seattle.
The panoramic bare landscape's Montana. For me, two
homes in one. More than that, consider how many here live
silent inside like my surrogate father. Don't laugh but
today I told my wife if I die here here's where I want
to be buried. She said, me too. I wish I could explain.
Something young inside me says when they visit my grave
I want grass moving sadly and the prolix sea in sight.
On the other hand, dead I won't give a damn. The Scots
are good at that too if that's what you prefer. They are
most accommodating, the Scots, most given to accepting
fate. To be good as these people are, you must have cruelty
deep in your history, must have tested your capacity
for hate long ago and know how bad it can be and what
it can do. There are castles of the cruel in ruin
and megalithic forts. The blood of our mothers has dried.
An old saying: The fate of the Gael is to lose everything.
From my upstairs window where every morning I write hard,
I see Uig pier across the bay. It reminds me
of a small dock years ago on a lake that didn't look

trouty and was. Remember? And these passionate gales
that stunt trees and leave grass bent permanently east
are the same force that took your dock. They're still taking
and still worth it. So what if it all burns out? It burns.
It is the fate of the Gael. It is the fate of the headless specter to be
forgotten by all. Once his howl was legend
on this island. Now I can't find a soul who knows him.
Not one. They stare at me when I ask. And only a few
old timers remember the water horse. And now what shall become
of us without monsters to pity and fear? The quest
for the autonomous man must have ended in this place
the day before the first tourist arrived. It was, as you
can't imagine, not the failure some scholars maintain,
you included. But you'd have to meet this wind head on
every day with no friend and no family and no
critical vocabulary before how alone we become
would hit home. The fate of the Gael is to lose. Everything
matters because everything dies and that includes storms.
It is calm. The sea does not stir. The hawk has no hard air
to hang on. Up on the moors, the autonomous man is lost
in this autonomous land. He does not answer our cry
to come home. When we light fires, he replies with the dark
silence of early warriors. Until he returns
he remains a threat to all of us who need others, who
need a good time on a dock catching trout, in a cottage
writing a poem for a friend far away. A new saying
I just made up: it is the fate of everyone to lose
the Gael. Five months to go and already I'm rehearsing
good bye, setting my weak mouth hard in the mirror, keeping
tears in check by thinking bad jokes. Did you hear the one
about the American who found so much quiet inside
he couldn't shut up, the way the lonely can't. I can. Dick.

Villager

What's wrong will always be wrong. I've seen him lean
against the house hours and glare at the sea. His eyes say
no boat will come. His harsh throated seemingly
good natured mother bends her back to the soil
and there at least all grows well. When I speak with him
his eyes move away to the sea and I imagine
the red in his face from drink is also from
some ancient tribal shame. To him I'm wealthy.
When we talk I know how wealthy I am.

The police have him on file: petty theft.
I'm certain he steals to make up for the nothing he finds
every day in the sea, and to find money for drink.
Some days a woman picks him up, a sister I'm told,
takes him away and hours later delivers him back
passed out. Next morning again he's propped against
the house, the tide out in his eyes. I imagine
his sister, if that's who she is, knows oblivion
is what he must have often to survive.

I have much to tell him. And nothing. I'd start
with the sea. I'd say, there was another sea something
like this long ago, and another me. By the time
I got to the point he'd be looking away and be right.
No two hurts are the same, and most have compensations
too lovely to leave. At night, a photo glows alive
inside him when his mother's asleep and the cops
aren't watching. It lights up in the dark
whenever he looks hard and by dawn has burned out.

I almost forget: he'd do anything for you. Love him
for what you might have become
and love him for what you are, not that far
from him. We are never that far. Love
everyone you can. The list gets longer and shorter.
We're seldom better than weather. We're nearly as good
as a woman we met in passing once at Invergarry.
Don't be sorry, for him or for self. Love the last star
broken by storm. And love you. You hold it together.

The Right Madness on Skye

Now I'm dead, load what's left on the wagon
and have the oxen move on. Tell absentee landlord driver,
Harry of Nothingham, slow. I want my last minutes on earth
filled with this island. For a long time
my days were nothing. My remarkable late surge
I attribute to fanciful chefs: cloud in the salad.
My dramatic reversal of fate insists on this will
read aloud in this poem this day of my death.
Have the oxen move on. Tell Harry of Nothingham, slow.

Take my body to Kilmuir cemetery and adorn
according to instructions. Don't forget the mint.
Carve any lines you want on my stone. If mine
double check spelling. I'm dumb. And triple check
high birds. Bring them down and make them state their names.
If none says 'Rhododendron' you know they're fakes.
Throw them out. Give the piper and drum five minutes
and explain to them, dead, I tire fast.
Have the oxen move on. Tell Harry of Nothingham, slow.

Alive, I often wounded my knee begging response.
My turn to put out. I will one eye to the blind of Dunvegan.
I will one ear to deaf salmon climbing the Conon.
And to the mute ocean I leave this haphazard tongue.
You might note on my stone in small letters:
Here lies one who believed all others his betters.
I didn't really, but what a fun thing to say.
And it's fun to be dead with one eye open in case
that stuck-up twitch in Arizona mourns my loss.

Toot, toot, lovers. Now that I'm moving ahead
you eagerly line the roadside to cheer these remains.
Some say, first, get rid of the body. Not me.
I say let the corpse dance. Make the living lie still.
I told you before, five minutes for piper and drum.
I leave vivid instructions and no one, no one listens.
Let's try it once more. I'm dead. I want to milk that wild
for all it's worth to the crowd already turning away.
Have the oxen move on. Tell Harry of Nothingham, slow.

By now you're no doubt saying, "We've got you to rights.
You can't write a poem from the grave."
Remember, I'm not buried. Only cold on the slab.
There's a hell of a difference between being stiff
from rigor mortis and being held rigid by peat.
Harry of Nothingham knows. Don't you, Harry old chap?
And oxen aren't as dumb as you think. Just because
I've no religion don't say heaven can't welcome me back
under the new majority quota now in effect.

Don't back up for cars. Clear the road for the dead.
Cry 'Fat bag of bones coming through.' I heard that note.
I told you, no trumpets. I told you, five minutes, no more
for piper and drum. Who's mouthing that organ for nothing?
Who's humming along and stamping the right time?
That's the wrong madness for Skye, I say. Wrong
for dispossessed crofters who didn't want me to die
and wrong for comedians waiting for final returns.
Have the oxen move on. Tell Harry of Nothingham, slow.

It's a long road that has no break in the blacktop.
It's a crock to say it. Are they really preparing a speech?
He was this, he was that, lies about me over
the open dirt? If so, have the oxen reverse.
Bring Harry of Nothingham back. I was rotten

in Denmark long before something caught the boat,
and I'm still non grata in Venice. Every time I level
the piper and drum drown me out.
Have the oxen move on. Tell Harry of Nothingham, slow.

If I'm allowed to digress this way, take me on tour.
What the hell. The hole that's waiting can wait.
I want a last look at Seattle and the way light
subtracts and adds miles to the journey.
And I want to ride again the road on the upper Rha.
If you've got a map you think I'm skipping about.
Listen. All places are near and far selves neighbors.
That wouldn't set well with scholars. Don't tell Harry.
Bury my wounded knee at Flodigarry.

Are we on course again? Good. Isle of Skye, right?
This the day of my death. Only feigned tears, like I ordered.
Make sure the flowers are plastic. Five minutes, remember,
piper and drum. Tell the nearly no mourners remaining
I was easy to mix up with weather. The weather
goes on. Me too, but right now in a deadly stiff line.
Tell the laird who tricked me into being a crofter
I never worked hard in my life except on a poem.
Have the oxen move on. Tell Harry of Nothingham, slow.

Tell Harry of Nothingham stop and have the oxen relax,
I want off at the crossroads. That's far as I go.
I was holding my breath all the time. Didn't I fool you?
Come on, admit it—that blue tone I faked on my skin—
these eyes I kept closed tight in this poem.
Here's the right madness on Skye. Take five days
for piper and drum and tell the oxen, start dancing.
Mail Harry of Nothingham home to his nothing.
Take my word. It's been fun.